Little and Happy! Dino's Best Birthday Ever

by Amelia Rice

Pictures by Yuliia Zolotova

Copyright 2021 by Amelia Rice - All rights reserved.

All Rights Reserved.

No part of this publication or the information in it may be quoted from or reproduced in any form by means such as printing, scanning, photocopying or otherwise without prior written permission of the copyright holder.

Disclaimer and Terms of Use:
Effort has been made to ensure that the information in this book is accurate and complete, however, the author and the publisher do not warrant the accuracy of the information, text and graphics contained within the book due to the rapidly changing nature of science, research, known and unknown facts and internet.

The Author and the publisher do not hold any responsibility for errors, omissions or contrary interpretation of the subject matter herein.

This book is presented solely for motivational and informational purposes only.

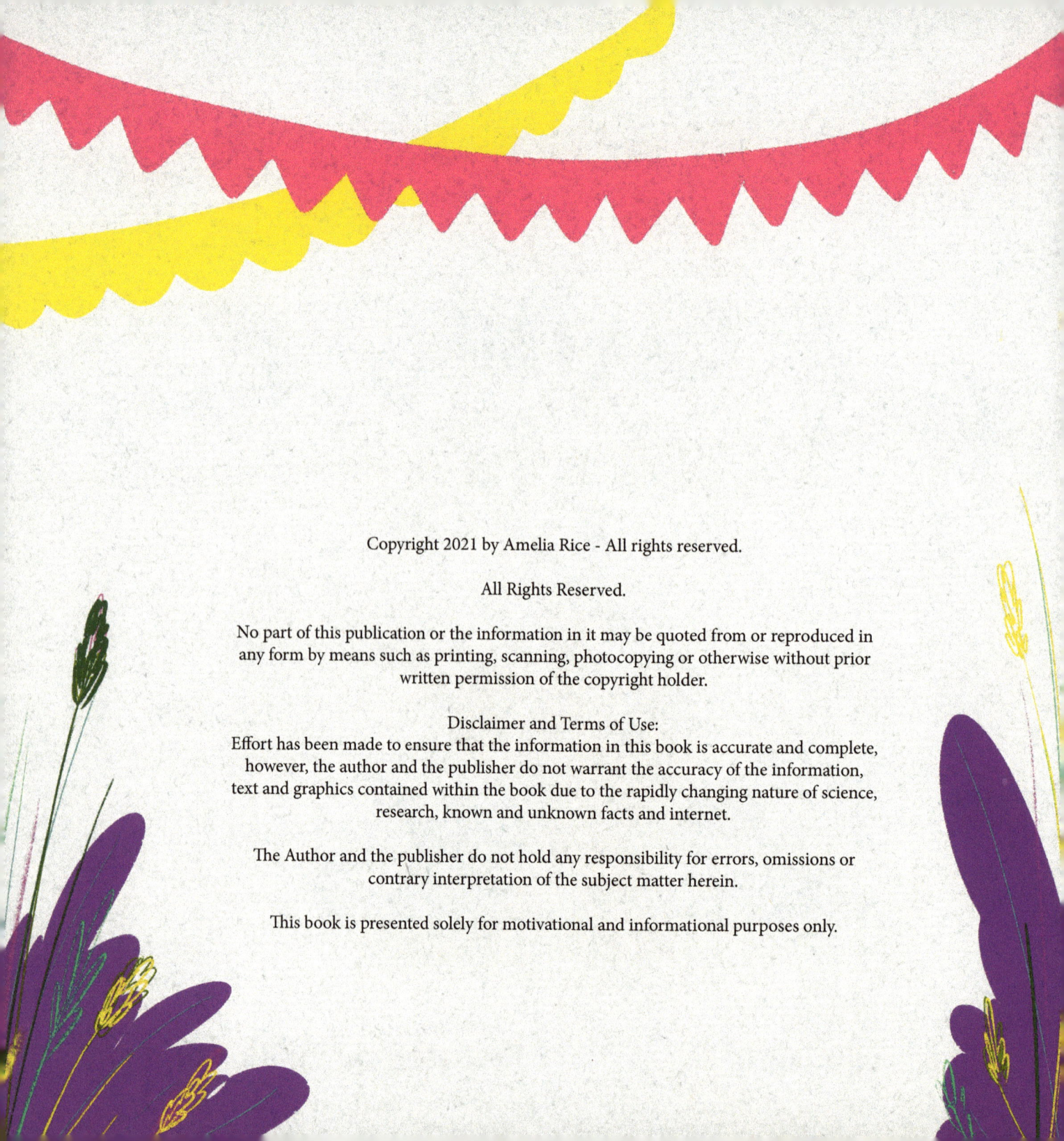

This book belongs to

_____

Little Dino skipped down the sidewalk with his hands in the air and a big smile on his face. It was his birthday, and he was planning the best birthday party ever!

All of his friends were coming and he wanted to make it extra special. As he walked, he thought about the cake, the decorations, the party games, and the balloons.
After all, what was a party without balloons?!

His first stop was Poppy's Balloon Shop. The store had every size and color of balloon you could imagine! There were star-shaped balloons, rainbow-colored balloons, and giant balloons that were almost as big as Little Dino!

"May I have five red balloons, please?" Little Dino asked. He was careful to say "please" and "thank you" just like his parents had taught him.

The store clerk smiled and handed him five red balloons. Dino was going to give one to each of his friends and keep one for himself. Little Dino paid for the balloons and skipped happily out of the store.

Next, Little Dino went to Confetti's Cake Shop. His mother had ordered a rocket-ship birthday cake with his name on it.
"Is my birthday cake ready?" asked Dino.
The baker smiled. "Yes it is! Would you like to see it?"

"No, thank you," Dino said. "I'll wait until my party. I want to be surprised!"
With that, the baker handed him the box with the cake in it and off Little Dino went.

His next stop was Jumpy's Fun Shop. Little Dino was going to pick out a jump house to put in the backyard. Balancing the cake and balloons, Little Dino walked inside and peered above the counter.

"What size jump house do you have for the best birthday party ever?" he asked.
The girl behind the counter showed him three different sizes.

There was a small jump house,
a medium-sized jump house,
and a super-deluxe jump house.
"I want the super-deluxe one, please!" Dino exclaimed.

The girl wrote down his address. "Your super-deluxe jump house will be delivered in time for your party!" she said. Little Dino smiled and waved goodbye.

Lastly, Little Dino walked to Gifty's Toy Shop. He went in and looked around. He wanted to pick out a party gift for his friends.
Hmm, he thought, *which party gift would be best?* He saw a box of colorful spin tops. The owner showed him how to twirl the top and make it spin across the floor. Wow! They were perfect! Little Dino bought five of them and went on his way.

Help Little Dino find his way home

When Little Dino got home, he spent the rest of the afternoon getting ready for the party. However, things did not go as planned.
When the jump house arrived, it was the smallest one! Little Dino could barely fit inside!

Then, one of the balloons popped when it brushed up against the cactus plant on the windowsill. "Oh no!" Dino shouted. "Now there are only four balloons!"

When Little Dino opened the box to see his cake, he saw that it said, "Happy Birthday Rhino!" instead of "Happy Birthday Dino!" And to make things worse, one of the spin tops wouldn't spin. Every time Little Dino twisted the top, it fell over.

Everything was going wrong! What was he going to do?

When Little Dino's friends arrived, they saw that he was very upset. They understood why when he showed them all the things that had gone wrong. Little Giraffe, who was always calm, said, "It will be okay, Little Dino. At least we are all together." Little Dog, who was full of energy, said, "We can play tag instead!"

Little Bear hugged Little Dino and said, "Don't worry. I was so clumsy at my birthday party, I dropped my cake in the dirt!"
Finally, Little Toucan, who was the funniest of the bunch said, "Cheer up, Little Dino! I'll pretend to be a spin top-see!"
With that, Little Toucan spun around and around, making his friends laugh.

Next, they took turns jumping in the jump house. Everyone got a turn.
They shared the balloons, hitting them back and forth until all of them popped!
And, they found a way to fix the broken spin top by working together and solving the problem.

A short time later, Little Dino and his friends sat around the table eating cake and having fun. "Look! I ate the piece that said "Rhino," Little Bear said. "And it was just as yummy as if it said "Dino!" Everyone laughed at their silly friend.

At the end of the day, Little Dino looked at all his friends and smiled from ear to ear. "Thank you for making this the best birthday party ever!" he exclaimed. "I didn't need the best cake, balloons, or games. All I need is best friends, like all of you!"

Scan QR code to get your bonus birthday invitation template for FREE!

Dear Reader,

Thank you so much for taking the time to read my book!

I know there are a lot of books out there,
and it means a great deal to me that you picked up one of mine.
I hope you enjoyed reading this book as much
as I enjoyed writing it.

I would really appreciate it if you could review my book.
Reviews, even very short ones, are a huge help to authors.
Here is the QR code «Little and Happy! Dino's Best Birthday Ever»
on Amazon:

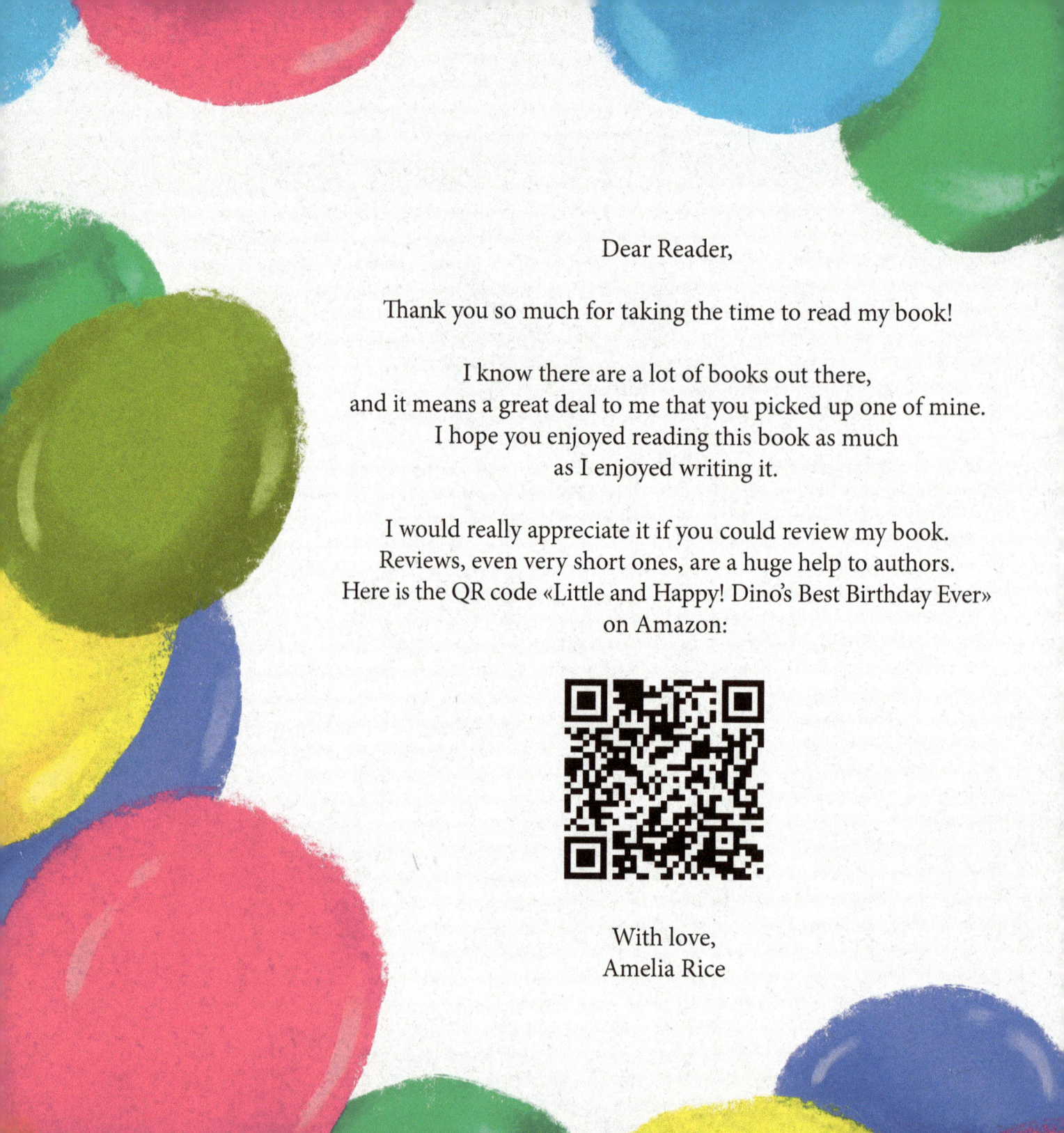

With love,
Amelia Rice